The Same and Different

Helen Hinchley

MARY GLASGOW PUBLICATIONS

These children are all alike in some ways.

In other ways they are different.

See how many similarities you can find.

See how many differences.

The children in this class are looking at some of the ways in which they are different.

How are they doing it?

What are they comparing?

What things do you think you could find to compare?

These are Natalie's, Danny's and Jerome's thumbprints.

Can you see the differences?

Hosein, Dawn and Shaima are going to make casts of their hands by pouring plaster into the clay moulds they have made. They will then be able to compare their hands.

Can you find ways of looking at parts of your bodies and comparing them?

Amy has to put her friends into sets. How many ways can Amy do this?

Could you put your friends into sets?

How many ways could you do it?

These children are trying to find out whose hands hold the most.

8 Can you think of any other ways of finding this out?

These children are trying to see who has the strongest grip.

Is this the best test?

Can you think of a better test?

The children are trying to find out who can jump furthest.

Is this a fair test?

Who can run fastest?

Is this the best way to find out?

Or is this way better?

Do you think you would need to do these tests more than once?

These children are trying to find out who has the strongest legs.

Why are they doing so many tests?

Would you need to do them all?

Can you think of any better ones?

Who can swim the furthest?

Here are some of the ways the children used to record the distances they swam.

What do you think of them?

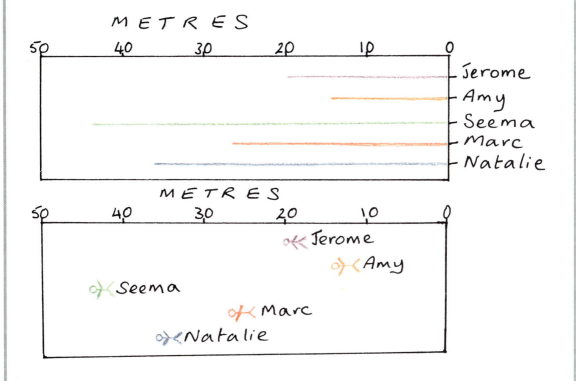

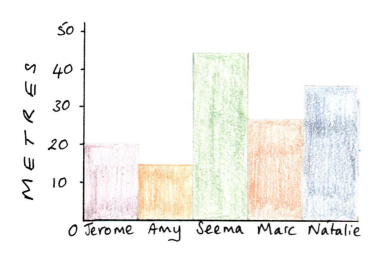

What can you find out about yourself and your friends?